Yagotosan Buddhist Series No.8

The Structure of Hindu Temples in Bali

Musashi Tachikawa
and
Sugeng Tanto

Published and Distributed 2025 by
ARM Corporation
3-1-12, Chiyoda, Naka-ku, Nagoya, Japan 460-0012
https://arm-p.co.jp

Cover design by Takeshi Kawamura
Editorial design by Hiroko Ishikawa, Editorial is

Under the auspices of
Yagotosan Buddhist Institute
c/o Kōshōji Temple, Yagoto, Showa-ku, Nagoya,
Japan 466-0825

©Authors, 2025, All right reserved.
No part of this book may be used or reproduced in any form or manner whatsoever
except for quotations or for use byEducational instituions without written permission of the authors.

ISBN 978-4-86333-217-1 C3014

Printed in Nagoya, Japan

Contents

Preface ……………………………………………………………………… i

Chapter 1   Introduction to Balinese Hinduism ………………………… 1

Chapter 2   The Outer Yard of Pura Puseh at Batuan Temple …………… 7

Chapter 3   Pura Desa and the House Temple……………………………. 39

Chapter 4   The Middle Yard of Pura Puseh……………………………… 51

Chapter 5   The Inner Yard of Pura Puseh ………………………………. 63

Chapter 6   Pura Dalem……………………………………………………. 97

Preface

Before I visited Bali for the first time in the summer of 1999, I knew from books that the island had a strong religious atmosphere. Upon arrival I was immediately fascinated by temple architecture, rituals, dance and music in Bali. Over the following ten years I visited the island several times. In 2001, I decided to do research on Batuan Temple in Batuan village, Gianyar district.

I was trained in Indian and Buddhist studies, not in Indonesian studies. I know neither the Indonesian language nor Balinese. Dr. Sugeng Tanto, an Indonesian scholar, joined me in 2002. In 2006 we published a preliminary report "Hindu Temples in a Village of Bali," as part of the results of a Japan Research Grant (No.14401003). I was (and am) envisioning a comparative study of the Hinduism in the Kathmandu Valley and the Hindu Dharma in Bali. Bali would be a Kathmandu in the sea; Kathmandu, a Bali surrounded by land.

In 2007, we discovered Hildred Geertz's *The Life of a Balinese Temple,* published in 2004, and suddenly our research on Batuan Temple seemed to have little meaning. In 2008 I took advantage of an opportunity to retake almost all the photos used in our 2006 report, but not long afterward we stopped working on the Bali project. A few years ago, I suddenly decided to publish an album of the 2008 Bali photos, which has become this book. We hope it will be of some help to those interested in the Hindu Dharma in Bali.

Many of the priests whom we originally consulted about the Hindu Dharma have now passed away. Sadly, I cannot meet and thank them directly, but let me thank their spirits. I take pleasure in being able to thank Mr. I Wayan Joni Artha, who kindly answered my questions during my most recent stay in Bali. Let me express my gratitude to Kathryn W. Sparling, Professor Emeritus, Carleton College, U.S.A., who revised the entire draft of this book. I would like to thank Mrs. Makiko Ito who has drawn illustrations used in this book. I am grateful to Yagotosan Kōshōji Temple, Nagoya, for publishing this book as

Yagotosan Buddhist Institute Series, No. 6, even though it deals basically with Hinduism.

    Finally, let me note that Batuan Temple seems in fact to have had some ancient connection with Buddhist tantrism. At the entrance to the head priests' residence of Batuan temple is a stone statue of Vairocana showing the *bodhy-agrī* gesture (excellent wisdom 智拳印) (see the photo on the back-cover). It is said to be one thousand years old.

Musashi Tachikawa
September 2024

Chapter 1

Introduction to Balinese Hinduism

Offerings. Pura Dalem Puri, Batuan

1 Hinduism on the Island of Bali

The Indonesian island of Bali is located several kilometers from the eastern edge of the island of Java. One can see Java from the western edge of Bali. The two cultures, however, are surprisingly different. Though Indonesia is an Islamic country, a particular kind of Hinduism is dominant in Bali. Bali State has a population of about three and half million, and more than eighty percent of the people are Hindus. It is only in Bali that Hinduism is prevalent in Indonesia.

Hinduism was introduced to Bali by Javanese Hindus, but Balinese Hinduism absorbed indigenous elements so that it became different from Indian Hinduism. In present day Bali, besides Hindus, one finds Muslims, Christians, Buddhists, and some who do not belong to any of these religions. In the northern part of the island, the number of Muslims is increasing. Bali Hindus call their religion "Hindu Dharma." Recently, Bali Hindus emphasize and seem to take increasing pride in their Dharma. This might be a reaction against the current rise in Islam.

Bali Hindus also call their religion "Āgama Tīrtha." The Sanskrit "āgama" means teaching or tradition. "Tīrtha" usually means the shore of a river, but in this case, it means sacred water. In the Indonesian language the adjective follows the noun. "Āgama Tīrtha" means the teaching of the sacred water, that is, the ambrosia that gives immortality not only to people but also to deities.

In Hindu rituals performed in Bali, priests dip a bundle of holy grass bound by thread into the sacred water and sprinkle the water over people's heads. The people are purified and sanctified by the water, without which any ritual is incomplete.

Bali Hinduism is considerably different from Indian Hinduism. Some scholars claim that what is called Hinduism in Bali is not Hinduism at all. With few exceptions, Hinduism in New York City, for example, the caste system has been a persistent, essential element of Hinduism. In Bali the caste system is substantially functioning. Furthermore, the orthodox Hindu pantheon has been adopted. Heroes from the Mahābhārata and the Rāmāyana often appear in theatrical performances. "Hinduism" in Bali may therefore be regarded as a kind of Hinduism. One sees other particular forms of Hinduism in other areas, for example among the Newar people in the Kathmandu Valley of Nepal.

Since most Balinese belong to the "low" caste, one does not see the strong antagonism evident, for example, in Pune, Maharashtra, where the Brahmana caste occupies a large portion of the entire population. However, the distinction between the high caste and the low caste sometimes does matter: The crematory differs according to the caste of the dead.

The Balinese believe in reincarnation, a core tenet of Hinduism. Performing dharma, i.e., justice and duty, is considered to lead to a better state (gati) in the next life. Accordingly, people have also accepted the thought of karma, if not so rigidly as in India.

On the other hand, ancestor worship in Bali is strong. Ancestor worship blends or coexists with belief in reincarnation. For example, after being purified by cremation and "the ritual of scattering ashes over sea or river" (mumukur), the spirit of the dead may come back to the house where they lived.

2 Batuan Temple in Batuan Village

In 1958 Bali became a separate province of Indonesia. The Indonesian government imposed an administrative system based on five levels: Negara (country), Propensi (province), Kabupaten (regency), Kecamatan (district), and Desa Adat (village). Bali has eight regencies (Jembrana, Tabanan, Badung, Gianyar, Klungkung, Bangli, Karangasem, Buleleng), and fifty-two districts. Each district has a number of villages (desa adat). The Sanskrit word "desa" (deśa) means a district or region, and the Indonesian word "adat" means conventional law.

Each desa adat has three Hindu temples: Pura Desa, Pura Puseh, and Pura Dalem. The Sanskrit word "pura" means castle/city enclosed by walls, but here it refers to a temple. Bali temples are usually surrounded by walls. Rituals for ancestors and regional deities are performed in Pura Desa. In Pura Puseh, they perform important rituals such as the annual commemoration of the temple's founding (odalan). Pura Dalem is used for death rituals.

The Desa Adat Batuan belongs to Gianyar District and is situated about ten kilometers northeast of Denpasar, the capital of Bali Province. Batuan village has a Pura Desa and a Pura Puseh, which are built together. However, the village has three separate Pura Dalem temples used by different castes. Pura Desa and Pura Puseh are found in a rectangular space enclosed by walls about fifty meters east to west and one hundred meters north to south.

Like other temples in Bali, each temple in Desa Adat Batuan contains a number of shrines. The structure of Pura Desa is simple, mainly because it is a small temple, as is usually the case. Pura Puseh, subsuming various shrines, is divided into three sections: outer yard, middle yard, and inner yard. Those three yards represent the leg, the belly, and the head of a deity. The scale of Pura Dalem is usually smaller than Pura Puseh, but larger than Pura Desa.

The main intent of this book is to show the structure of each pura of Batuan Temple in Batuan village. The outer yard of Pura Puseh, Batuan, is treated in Chapter Two. The Pura Desa of Batuan Temple is dealt with in Chapter Three. The middle yard of Pura Puseh is explained in Chapter Four and the inner yard of Pura Puseh is treated in Chapter Five. Chapter Six examines the three temples of Pura Dalem in Batuan village.

Fig. 1.1 Map of Desa Adat Batuan, from Kantor Perbekel (village office) of Desa Adat Batuan, Sukawati, Gianyar.

3   Rituals in Bali

In Bali, a common term referring to ritual is upacara, which comes from the Sanskrit word "upacāra," meaning offerings or the action of offering to deities.   In India or Nepal, the word "pūjā" more generally refers to an offering service to deities. "Upacāra" and "pūjā" are basically interchangeable: The compound "Upacāra-pūjā" is often used. In Bali, the term "pūjā" is also sometimes used in the sense of "upacara."

In India/Nepal, the offering service (upacara, pūjā) requires the following procedure: A deity (or deities) is invoked and called to the place where the ritual is to be performed. Then the deity is entertained as a guest. The deity is bathed and given new clothes. After food is offered, the deity returns home. Offering services are performed this way in Bali as well.

In Inda and Nepal, the Offering Service in Sixteen Steps (ṣodaśa-upacāra-pūjā) is the well-known model for Hindu offering services. The sixteen steps are as follows:

1. Invocation to the deity
2. Offering a seat
3. Offering water for washing the feet of the deity
4. Offering sacred water
5. Offering water for rinsing the mouth of the deity
6. Bathing
7. Offering the lower garment (vastra)
8. Offering the upper garment (upavastra)
9. Offering fragrant materials (gandha)

10. Offering flowers
11. Offering incense
12. Offering a lamp
13. Offering food
14. Circumambulating the divine image clockwise
15. Salutation to the deity
16. Seeing off the departing deity

The name "Offering Service in Sixteen Steps" is rarely used in Bali. An offering service in Bali has virtually the same structure as Indo-Nepali pūjā. It begins with the invocation to the deity, who is guided to stay temporally in one shrine, then invited to move to another shrine, then asked to yet another shrine. Arriving at the main shrine, called Pengias Agung, the deity is dressed up and adorned. This procedure approximates the seventh and eighth steps of the Offering Service in Sixteen Steps. Having changed clothes, the deity is then invited to the shrine named Pengaruman (scented place), which is generally built close to Pengias Agung, in order to receive offerings. This procedure corresponds to the thirteenth step of the Offering Service in Sixteen Steps. Having receiving offerings, the deity returns home. The priests and the people see the deity off.

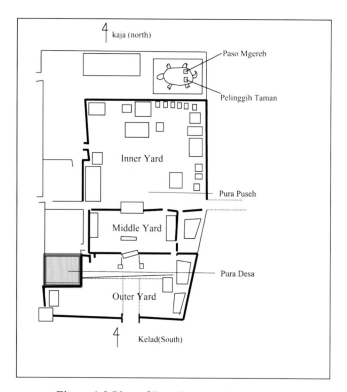

Figure 1.2 Plan of Pura Desa and Pura Puseh

Chapter 2

The Outer Yard of Pura Puseh at Batuan Temple

Saraswati Festival, Batuan

2.1 The Gates of Pura Puseh

Pura Puseh of Batuan Temple has two main gates: a split gate known as Candi Bentar and a tower gate called Kori Agung. Both are based on the image of a mountain. They are, however, different in design and function. Candi Bentar is an elaborately carved tower sliced into two halves; Kori Agung has the form of an acute triangle. Candi Bentar is used to enter the outer yard of the temple (nista mandala), while Kori Agung is a symbolic gate to the inner yard (uttama mandala). Visitors cannot enter through Kori Agung gate, as it is almost always closed. There is another entrance to the inner yard at the left side of Kori Agung. The style of Candi Bentar and Kori Agung is apparently derived from ancient temples (candi) in Java. The split form of Candi Bentar can be seen in East Java even today.

Fig. 2.1 Gate Candi Bentar. Batuan temple was established by Minister (patih) Kebo Iwa in 944 Saka (1016 AD).

Fig. 2.2 Bamboo pillar (penjor) used in recently performed rituals, in front of Candi Bentar.

Fig. 2.3 Bale Kulkul (Pavilion of Wooden Bells) is seen at the southeast corner of the wall; statues of eleven guardian deities protect the southern wall. This photo was taken in February 2010. The bushes seen in Fig. 2.1 (Photo taken in 2008) are not here.

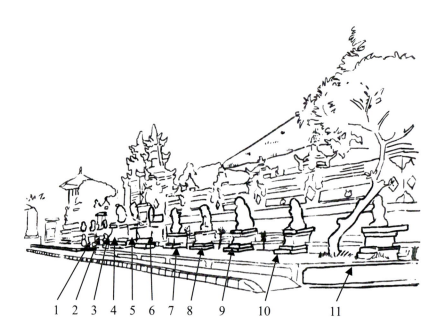

Fig. 2.4 Eleven statues in front of the southern wall. The following eleven statues (1-11) stand in front of the southern wall from viewer's left to right (Figs. 2.5-15). For example, number 1 in Fig. 2.4 corresponds to Fig.2.5; number 2 in Fig. 2.4, to Fig.2.6 and so forth.

Fig. 2.5 Guardian Merdah

Fig. 2.6 Guardian Malen

Fig. 2.7 Guardian Ngada

Fig. 2.8 Prasta, attendant of Demon Rahwana in the *Rāmāyana*

Fig. 2.9 Guardian Prahasta

Fig. 2.10 Guardian Dumaraksa or Destarata

Fig. 2.11 Guardian Raksasa Gundul

Fig. 2.12 Guardian Delem

Fig. 2.13 Guardian Kala

Fig. 2.14 Guardian deity Prasta

Fig. 2.15 Guardian Sangut (The names of these eleven guardians follow Geertz [2004: 135]

2.2 Bale Kulkul (Pavilion of Wooden Bells)

Fig. 2.16 House Temple of the Pande Family (viewer's left) and Bale Kulkul. A statue of Guardian Raksasa stands in front of the House Temple (cf. Fig. 2.17).

Fig. 2.17
The back of the Raksasa statue seen in the center of Fig. 2.16. According to the inscription on The base of the statue, it was installed on September 19,1985.

Fig. 2.18 The front of Raksasa standing before the house temple of the Pande Family (cf. Fig. 2.15)

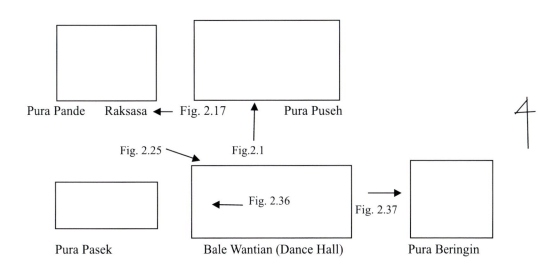

Fig. 2.19 Location of Pura Pande, Pura Puseh, Bale Wantian, and other buildings.

Fig. 2.20 Bale Kulkul (Pavilion of Wooden Bells). Three wooden bells are seen under the roof.

Three wooden bells are usually hung inside the pavilion (bale), which rests on four pillars with a thatched or tiled roof. The sound of wooden bells conveys various messages, such as a village wedding, grief at the death of a resident, or fire emergency. The bells also guide people through ritual procedures. Creatures such as Bhoma (demon faces), lions, Garuda, and elephants are depicted on the walls of the pavilion.

Fig. 2.21 Bhoma depicted on the lower part of Bale Kulkul. Balinese believe that Bhoma keeps evil away.

The name Bhoma (born from land) derives from the legend of Siva (Siwa)'s appearance from a gigantic linga (*Vāyupurāṇa*, 55.13-57; *Liṅgapurāṇa*, 1.17.32-59; *Kūrmapurāṇa*, 1.25.67-101). Brahma and Visnu, seeing an extraordinarily high pillar burning in front of them, began to argue over who held the superior power. The two deities wanted to find the top and the bottom of the burning pillar. Brahma, changing his form into a bird, flew up to discover the height of the luminous pillar; however, he could not reach the top. Wisnu, assuming his boar form, burrowed down into the earth, but he could not see the bottom of the linga. When the two bewildered gods returned exhausted to the earth, Siva appeared from the flaming linga (cf. [Kramrish 1981: 159]).

The Indian legend has been elaborated in Bali. The story of Bhoma can be related to God Wisnu and Mother of the Earth, Sang Hyang Wasundari (Skt. vasumdharī). In Sanskrit, what is born from bhūmi (earth) is called "bhauma," spelled bhoma in Bali. Sang Hyang Wasundari, the deity of the earth, is Bhoma's mother. His father is Wisnu.

Here is the common Balinese version of the Indian legend: Brahma and Wisnu once competed to see who was more powerful. Producing a great force in heaven, Brahma took the form of Garuda. He wanted to fly up to the summit of heaven. Wisnu turned himself into a boar and began to burrow into the earth. He wanted to demonstrate his power. When he reached the bottom of the earth, he met Wasundari, the goddess of the earth, and pursued her. She became pregnant and gave birth to a son Bhoma, who is believed to reside in all trees and plants on earth. It is well known that Wisnu is closely connected with water. One of the many epithets of Wisnu is "Nārāyana," whose abode (āyana) is water (nārā). Balinese believe that life is born when water meets the earth [Davison 2003: 38].

In Balinese temple buildings, Bhoma appears only in the form of a face. He has no limbs. He has the form of a lion-faced demon called Kīrtimukha, known all over Asia, traceable to Syria and Babylonia. The demon seems to have two origins: Medusa in Greek mythology and the lion-face seen in ancient Syrian ritual vessels.

Fig. 2.22 Bale Kulkul (viewer's left) and the southern wall (part)

Fig. 2.23 The southern wall showing faces of Saes. In front of the wall is the image of Guardian Deity Merdah.

Fig. 2.24 The eastern half of the southern wall. One may see a Sae in the center of the photo.

There are ten images (Fig. 2.25-34) of Sae on the southern wall. Following are ten images, from viewer's left to right. Sae always holds leaves, sometimes with both hands; while Bhoma has neither leaves nor hands.

Fig. 2.25 Sae 1 (without hands)

Fig. 2.26 Sae 2 (without hands)

Fig. 2.27 Sae 3 (without hands)

Fig. 2.28 Sae 4 (without hands)

Fig. 2.29 Sae 5 (without hands)

Fig. 2.30 Sae 6 (with hands)

Fig. 2.31 Sae 7 (without hands)

Fig. 2.32 Sae 8 (with hands)

Fig. 2.33 Sae 9 (without hands)

Fig. 2.34 Sae 10 (with hands)

2.3 Bale Wantilan (Event Hall, Large Wall-kess Pavilion)

Fig. 2.35 Event hall (Bale Wantilan) in front of the main gate Candi Bentar.

Fig. 2.36 Stage at Bale Wantilan. Ritual dances are performed in this hall.

Fig. 2.37 Pura Beringin near Bale Wantilan. Beringin (Ficus microcarpa) is often worshipped as a deity in Bali. Here a deified Beringin tree grows in a small shrine (pura) with an enclosing wall. A Beringin tree is often planted at the center of a village, signifying the center of the world.

Fig. 2.38 Pelinggih Ratu Tumpek (viewer's left) and Pelinggih Ratu Waringin in Pura Pelinggih (cf. Fig. 2.37)

2.4 Candi Kurung and Bale Agung (Large Hall)

Fig. 2.39 Candi Kurung of Pura Puseh seen through the split gate of Candi Bentar.
The cut surfaces of Candi Bentar are without carving, as if sliced by a sword.

Like other temples, Pura Puseh of Batuan Temple has three yards: outer, middle and inner. Through Gate Candi Bentar one enters the outer yard of Pura Puseh. The outer yard is a space for social gatherings and ritual preparations. Before entering the outer yard, one purifies the mind. Preparations for rituals are made in the middle yard. Important or large rituals are performed in the inner yard, where main shrines, altars, storage and the mount Meru tower are found. Some shrines in the inner yard serve as temporary residing places for deities visiting the temple.

Fig. 2.40 Bale Gong (Music Hall) behind the southern wall of Pura Puseh

Fig. 2.41 Bale Wantilan (viewer's left), Bale Kulkul, and Bale Agung (Large Hall), southeast corner of the outer yard

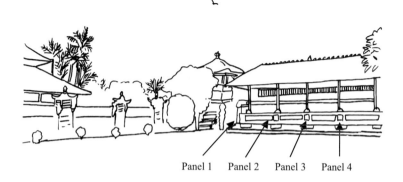

Fig. 2.42 Bale Wantilan (viewer's left), Bale Kulkul (center), and Bale Agung

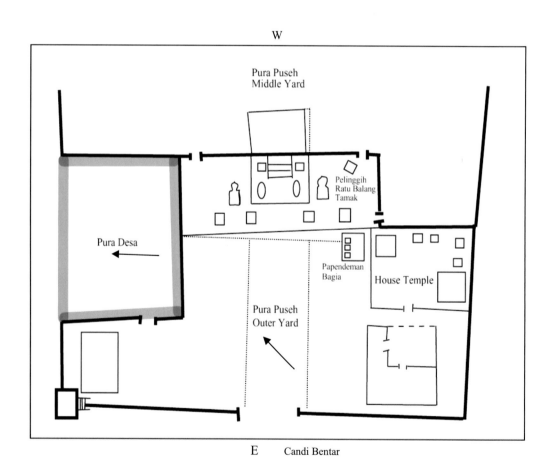

Fig. 2.43 Plan of Pura Puseh Outer Yard

Fig. 2.44 Bale Agung (Large Hall). Four relief panels depicting Tantri stories are attached to the lower wall of the hall (Figs. 2.41-44).

A series of stories-within-a-story, called the Tantri stories, are well known both in Bali and in Java. Every night Diah Tantri, a beautiful and wise daughter from a noble family, relates a different animal fable to the king to whom she has been given. Most of her stories are didactic, offering advice about self-control, awareness, and friendship.

Fig. 2.45 Panel 1 illustrating an animal fable (Fig. 2. 42). Sae (or Bhoma) is depicted in the center of the panel (see Figs. 2.25-34). Sae (or Bhoma) is believed to keep evil away from sacred areas such as the Large Hall. Bhoma has both upper and lower tusks; Sae does not have lower tusks.

Fig. 2.46 Panel 2 (Fig. 2. 42)

Fig. 2.47 Panel 3 (Fig. 2. 42)

Fig. 2.48 Panel 4 (Fig. 2. 42)

Fig. 2.49 Bale Agung (Large Hall, viewer's left) seen side by side with Pura Desa. Bale Agung is a meeting place (paruman) for priests.

Fig. 2.50 Bale Agung (viewer's left) and Pura Desa

As mentioned before, every village (adat) has three temples: Pura Desa, Pura Puseh and Pura Dalem. Pura Desa is dedicated to Brahma. Pura Puseh is dedicated to Wisnu (Skt. Viṣṇu), who is associated with the irrigation systems according to the Bali tradition. Pura Dalem is the temple for Siwa (Śiva), who is believed to be the destroyer of the world. Death rituals are performed in this temple. These three are the main deities of Indian Hinduism. The Goddess Saraswati is worshipped as the consort of Brahma. Parvati, the most beloved consort of Siwa, is well known in Bali. Skanda and Ganesa, the children of Siwa and Parvati, are also popular.

Since the Balinese worship the three main Hindu deities as well as other important gods, one might expect Bali Hinduism to have the same structure as Indian Hinduism. The Hinduism in Bali may indeed be under the canopy of Indian Hinduism, but the reality of Bali Hinduism under that canopy is considerably different from Indian Hinduism.

Fig. 2.51 Relief panel depicting the story of Sutasoma, found on the northern wall of Bale Agung

The story of Sutasoma is depicted on the northern wall of Bale Agung. This is a Buddhist Jataka story originating in India. The Sutasoma story was revised in Java in the fourteenth century, and the revised version became popular in Bali.

It tells of the self-sacrifice of a Bodhisatva named Sutasoma, once born as a prince in the royal house in Kuru country, Indraprastha (India). This prince was a model of good conduct, learning, mercy, modesty, and wisdom.

"Sutasoma" literally means squeezed soma juice (or wine). "Suta" is the past participle of the verb "√su" (to squeeze), and "soma" probably means juice squeezed from a kind of mushroom. After drinking Soma juice, priests became intoxicated, so that their voices sounded more impressive to the patrons observing the ritual.

That is the usual meaning of soma. The "soma" of Sutasoma, however, refers to the moon, which, in contrast with the hot sun, symbolizes someone cool, gentle, serene. In Indian literature the moon is often a metaphor for a beautiful face. In Bali, the prefix 'su,' (good) suggests the good behavior of the prince.

In the Himalayan district there lived a man-eating king named Kalmapasada. Once he injured his leg, which did not heal for a long time. He swore to offer up the lives of one hundred kings, hoping that the Deity Kala would cure him. Kalmapasada captured one hundred kings. Kala, however, would not accept those lives, demanding that Sutasoma be offered instead.

Powerful as he was, Sutasoma did not use his strength to oppose Kalmapasada. With mercy and a peaceful mind, he subdued Kalmapasada and freed all the princes. Sutasoma taught Kalmapasada the right way to live as a king.

Fig. 2.52 Bale Agung. Elephants (gajah) (cf. Fig. 3.11), Garuda and lions are depicted on a corner of the tower.

Fig. 2.53 Kori Agung gate (Candi Kurung)

Candi Kurung is situated on the border between the outer yard and the middle yard. The outer yard is considered to be less sacred than the other yards. In the outer yard preparations for the main rituals are made. When a large ceremony is held, deities are first invited to Candi Kurung and then to other shrines. Deities are treated with offerings and entertained with music and dance. All this is usually done in the outer yard. When the ritual is over, the deities return home.

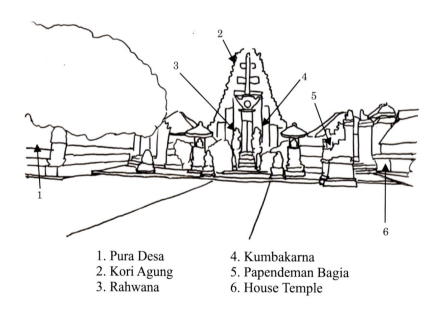

1. Pura Desa
2. Kori Agung
3. Rahwana
4. Kumbakarna
5. Papendeman Bagia
6. House Temple

Fig. 2.54 Statues and House Temple in front of Kori Agung

To the viewer's left of Kori (Candi) Agung is a statue of Rahvana (3); to the viewer's right, a statue of Kumbakarna. The closed gate Kori Agung, which leads deities to the inner yard, is guarded by Raksasas and Nagas. This massive gate is similar in design to Candi Bentar (Fig. 2.39), but it is raised high off the ground.

Fig. 2.55 Shrine called Sedahan Apit Lawang (Split Gate Offering), on the viewer's left of Kori Agung. This is also called Semar shrine.

Fig. 2.56 Sedahan Apit Lawang to viewer's right of Kori Agung.
This is also called Togog shrine.

Togog is one of the clown servants to the Kurawa (Kaurava Princes) appearing in the Javanese and Balinese versions of the *Mahābhārata*. Some scholars claim that Togog is a brother of Semar, an adviser to Pandawas.

Fig. 2.57 Naga in front of Candi Kurung

Temples are often guarded by animals such as lions or birds. Snakes (naga) are also reliable guards of temples or shrines. Balinese have respected snakes as deities from ancient times. Through more than one thousand years, Balinese ideas have merged with the Indian mythological image of snakes. The Balinese snake deity began to be called by the Indian name Anantabhoga (see Fig. 5.36). This Naga was symbolically buried in the Bali earth, and his head is believed to be situated at the center of the island.

Fig. 2.58 Bhoma on the wall of Kori Agung (cf. Fig. 2.21)

Fig. 2.59 Rahvana (viewer's left) and Kumbakarna

Fig. 2.60 Four guardians in front of Kori Agung

Fig. 2.61 Guardian 1 (viewer's far left)

Fig. 2.62 Guardian 2 (second from left)

Fig. 2.63 Guardian 3

Fig. 2.64 Guardian 4 (far right)

Fig. 2.65 Shrine Papendeman Bagia (Buried Happiness). This shrine rests on a foundation stone of the temple. The shrine plays an important role in the commemoration of the temple's founding (odalan).

Fig. 2.66 Detail of Figure 2.61. The image in the center is Pendeta, founder of the temple. The energy of Shrine Papendeman Bagia is renewed every twenty-five years.

Chapter 3

Pura Desa and the House Temple

Priest at Poedan, Saraswati Festival, Batuan Temple

3.1 Pura Desa

Batuan Temple has two enclosed temples. Pura Desa, occupying a small area, is attached to Pura Puseh (see Fig. 2.51). Fig. 3.1 shows the entrance gate to Pura Desa.

Fig. 3.1 Statue of Sahadewa to viewer's left of the entrance gate to Pura Desa; and statue of Rangda, an incarnation of Durga, to viewer's right of the entrance gate (photographed September 2010)

Fig. 3.2 Woman making daily offering to deities enshrined in Pura Desa

Sahadewa was a good and loyal son of Queen (dewi) Kunti. One day a witch cast a spell over her. Under the power of the spell, Queen Kunti became angry with Sahadewa, and she condemned him to death. Sahadewa was tied to a tree and left as the prey of Durga, the goddess of death. Siwa rescued Sahadewa and gave him immortality. Durga took the form of a fearsome long-haired demon and, with a blood-curdling shriek, flew up to the sky. Next Durga began to perform her dance of death, as she does whenever she intends to kill. Try as she might, however, she was unable to kill Sahadewa, thanks to the immortality granted him by Siwa.

Durga's servant, Goddess Kalika (Kālikā), threatened Sahadewa. Kalika became infuriated and transformed herself first into a wild boar, then into Garuda, and finally into Rangda in order to attack Sahadewa. The magical power of Rangda was so strong that Sahadewa then summoned the lion-faced hero Barong. Barong and Rangda engaged in a fierce, endless battle. Rangda represents the force of darkness; Barong, that of light.

Fig. 3.3 A woman (cf. Fig. 3.2) making offerings to deities in Pengias (Hall for Adorning), where deities are supposed to change clothes in order to receive the offerings. "Pengias" means to change clothes or put on ornaments.

Fig.3.4 Shrines in Pura Desa: Pengias (viewer's left) and Pengaruman Ratu Desa

Fig.3.5 Shrines in Pura Desa (cf. Fig. 3.6).

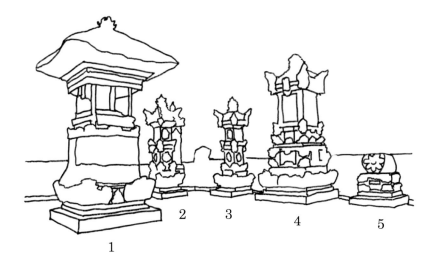

Fig. 3.6 Shrines in the yard of Pura Desa

1. Pengaruman Ratu Desa	Scented place for village deities (Ratu Desa). "Pen" is a prefix, "garu" (arum) means to scent, and "man" indicates a place. Ratu means a deity.
2. Pesimpangan Ratu Batukaru	Place for temporary stay of Queen (ratu) Batukaru. "Simpang" means a place for the temporary stay. "Pe" is a prefix. "Simpang" originally meant to move from one place to another. A house or residence is prepared at the border of two districts. Pesimpangan is a shirine where deities are invited to stay awhile before crossing the border. Villagers offer temporary abode to deities from a distant district. "Ratu" means deity. Ratu Batukaru is said be a deity worshipped at the base of Agung mountain, where some families of Batuan village originated.
3. Pesimpangan Ratu Batur	Place for temporary stay for Deities of Batur district. The ancestors of some people of Batuan village are said to have come from Batur district, which is near Agun mountain.
4. Gedong Ngelurah Gumi	Shrine for the security deity Gumi (earth). "Gedong" means a kind of deity; "ngelurah," security.
5. Batu Alam	"Batu" means a stone; "alam," natural. A sprit is believed to reside in this stone.

Fig. 3.7 Pengaruman Ratu Desa.

As mentioned in Chapter 1, the three deities Brahma, Wisnu and Siwa are worshipped in Bali as they are in Indian Hinduism. Pengaruman Ratu Desa is a scented place for village deities. "Ratu Desa" indicates village deities. Pengaruman Ratu Desa is dedicated to Brahma. We see that Bali Hinduism (Hindu Dharma) is a synthesis of Bali indigenous religion and Indian Hinduism.

Fig.3.8 Brahma drawn on the front panel of Pengaruman shrine. Here Brahma is depicted smelling a flower.

Fig. 3.9 Saraswati drawn on the reverse side of the Brahma panel (Fig. 3.8). In Bali Saraswati is considered to be Brahma's consort. Here she is depicted riding a swan. In India, the vehicle of Brahma and of his spouse is a goose (haṃsa).

Fig.3.10 Pesimpangan Ratu Batukaru. Sae (middle) and two Makaras are depicted on the shrine base. In Bali, Makara is also called Karang Gajah. "Gajah" means elephant. On the island, Makara is often considered to be an elephant.

The origin of Makara may to traced back to the ancient myth of Capricorn, half goat, half fish. In the course of its thousand-mile journey from Greece and Egypt to Asia, Makara changed its form: from whale to crocodile-like animal, bird, then fish. When it reached Indonesia, Makara became a mythical creature with a long proboscis. This Makara. who lives in the ocean, is said to have created all living beings in this world.

3. 2 The House Temple in the Outer Yard

In Bali there are two kinds of house temples. Merajan is the house temple of higher castes (Brahmana and Ksatria). Sanggah is a family or private temple for people belonging to the other castes. The structure of these two kinds of temples is similar, and the deities enshrined are almost identical. Each family temple contains shrines dedicated to the family's deified ancestors.

Ancestor worship is the core of Balinese Hinduism. People believe that the spirits of their ancestors significantly influence their daily lives. In order to dispel evil and bring good luck, people treat their ancestors' spirits courteously. If people perform ancestor worship properly and with care, ancestors will, in turn, protect them in this world.

Fig.3.11 House Temple (viewer's left) and Bale Gong (Music Hall).
"Gong" means a round metal drum.

Fig.3.12 Shrines in the House Temple, which belongs to a Sudra family affiliated with Batuan Temple. From the viewer's left: Gedung Jog, Arip-arip, Padmasari, Gedong Penyimpanan, Ratu Ngelurah, and Pengias the main shrine of the family temple.

Fig.3.13 Two shrines: Arip-arip (viewer's left) and Padmasari (right) found in the House Temple (photo taken during the Galungan festival, January 2004)

Chapter 4

The Middle Yard of Pura Puseh

People praying at Saraswati Festival, Batuan Temple

4.1 The Middle Yard

In the middle yard of Pura Puseh are found Bale Pesantia (Peaceful Hall), Aling Aling (Partition Wall) and Bale Dana Punia (Merit-Giving Hall). This yard, representing the belly of a deity, is used mainly for preparation for rituals, such as arranging offering materials. Fig. 4.1 shows the placement of the shrines and the wall in the yard.

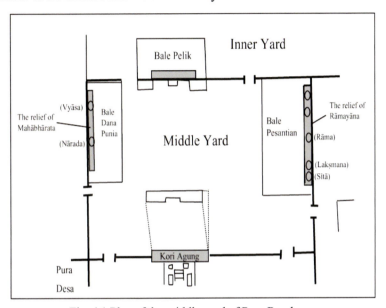

Fig. 4.1 Plan of the middle yard of Pura Puseh

Fig. 4.2 The back side of the entrance to the middle yard (viewer's right).
On the left, the house where offerings are prepared.

Fig. 4.3 Bale Pesantian (Peaceful Hall), where offerings are placed temporarily. There is a relief on the wall (Fig. 4.4-5).

Fig. 4.4 Section, viewer's left, of the panel on the wall of Bale Pesantian. The panel depicts an episode from the Ramayana, in which Rama's wife Sita was thrown into a fire to test her purity. Since she was not burned, she proved herself to be pure.

Fig. 4.5 Middle section of the panel. The man standing in the center and the man sitting next to him seem to be Rama and Laksmana, younger brother of Roma.

Fig. 4.6 Right section of the panel. The man kneeling in the center is Laksmana; the man standing near him is Rama.

Fig. 4.7 Aling aling (partition wall) in the middle yard, preventing evil spirits from invading the inner part of the temple

Fig. 4.8 Back of Kori Agung seen from the entrance gate to the inner yard

Fig. 4.9 Back of Kori Agung, where Bhoma (Kala Bhoma, cf. Figs. 2.21, 2.54), lions, and Makaras are depicted.

Fig. 4.10 Aling Aling (partition wall) built behind Kori Agung (cf. Figure 4.7)

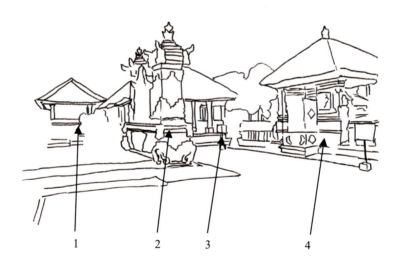

Fig. 4.11 Aling Aling Wall in the middle yard and Bale Pelik in the inner yard

    1. Kitchen (suci) located outside the middle yard
    2. Wall called Paduraksa behind Kori Agung (Fig. 4.1)
    3. Bale Dana Punia
    4. Bale Pelik

Fig. 4.12 Dhanawa holding a sword? He punishes evil deeds. According to Geertz [2004: 134], this is a statue of Raksasa Panca Maha Buta.

Dhanawa, originally an evil spirit, later became a virtuous being. He is believed to protect temples. Here (Fig. 4.12) Dhanawa is enshrined in a niche in Aling Aling Wall. According to a Bali tradition, Dhanawa poisoned the drinking water, causing general calamity. The Balinese prayed to Indra for help. Indra subdued the demon and shot an arrow into the earth, and the water became clean.

Fig. 4.13 According to a pemangku in charge of the temple, this statue is of a priest (pedanda) reciting mantras. The head decoration reminds us of Siwa, and the face is similar to that of Dhanawa (cf. Fig. 4.12). According to Gieertz [2004:133], this is Rawana.

Fig. 4.14 Bale Dana Punia (Merit-Giving Hall). "Dana" (Skt. dāna) means giving; "punia" (Skt. puṇya), merits, good health, beauty, etc.

Fig. 4.15 Panel on the wall of Bale Dana Punia, depicting episodes from the Mahabharata

Fig. 4.16 Left section of Fig. 4.15

Fig. 4.17 Right section of the panel (Fig. 4.15.). Wiyasa (viewer's right) is giving advice to court ladies. From viewer's left to right: Yana (mother of Irawan), Drupadi (Draupadī), Irawan, and Bagawan Wiyasa.

Chapter 5

The Inner Yard of Pura Puseh

Priest giving sacred water to villagers
at Saraswati Festival

5.1 Shrines in the Inner Yard

A number of shrines and storehouses have been built in the Inner Yard. At times of rituals, deities are invited to this yard, where they change clothes in the Main Hall (Pengias Agung) in order to receive offerings.

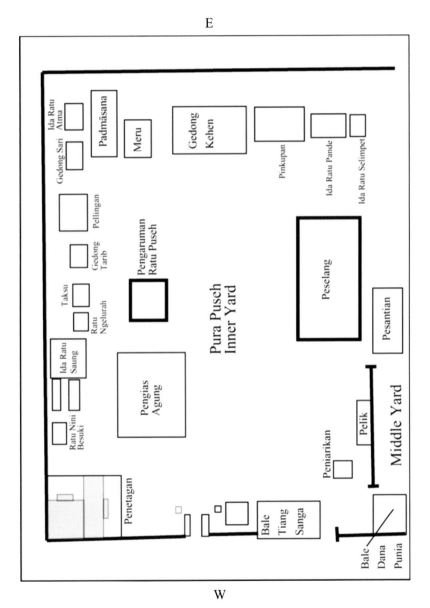

Fig. 5.1 Plan of the Inner Yard of Pura Puseh

Fig. 5.2 Bale Penyarikan (viewer's right). Atop this shrine is Siwa Lingga (Skt. liṅga). Here offerings (canang) have been placed before the Lingga. The hall to viewer's left is Bale Tian Sanga (Hall of Nine Pillars), where priests rest before performing rituals.

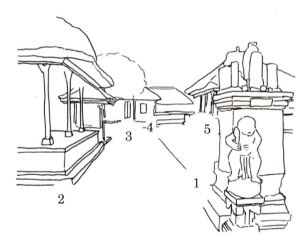

Fig. 5.3 View of the western side of the inner yard

1. Bale Penyarikan. This shrine commemorates the activities of visitors to the temple.
2. Bale Tiang Sanga
3. Poedan
4. Bale Gong
5. Pengias Agung

Fig. 5.4 Lingga of Bale Penyarikan. Offerings are placed in a bowl made of palm leaves.

Fig .5.5 Bale Tiang Sanga (center) and Poedan (viewer's right, cf. Fig. 5.7)

Fig. 5.6 Garuda image on a beam on the underside of the Bale Tiang Sanga roof.

Fig. 5.7 Poedan, where a priest (pemangku) conducts rituals such as Upacara Sarasvati (Skt. sarasvatīpūjā). The original meaning of "poedan" seems to be related to Vedic chanting.

Fig. 5.8 Poedan immediately before an offering service to Saraswati (September 2006)

Fig. 5.9 Entrance on the western side of Pura Puseh. This entrance is used as an alternative gate when large or important rituals are performed.

Fig. 5.10 View from the northern side of the inner yard. From the viewer's left, Pelik (Fig. 5.58), Kori Agung (Fig. 2.49), Bale Penyarikan (Fig. 5.2), Bale Dana Punia (Fig. 4.14), Bale Tiang Sanga (Fig. 5.5,9), and Poedan (Fig. 5.7-9)

Fig. 5.11 From the viewer's left, Tian Sanga, Poedan, Bale Gong, and part of Pangias Hall (Main Hall)

Fig. 5.12 Bale Gong, where musical instruments are stored. Gamelan music is performed during rituals on the stage of this hall (bale).

Fig. 5.13 Kala Bhoma depicted above the southern door of Bale Gong

Fig. 5.14 Saraswati on the western door of Bale Gong

Balinese worship Saraswati as the goddess of knowledge and learning. She embodies the free flow of wisdom and consciousness. Often she holds a sacred scripture in one main hand and a lotus, the symbol of true knowledge, in the other. With her other two hands she plays the music of love on the Veena. She is dressed in white, symbolizing purity. Her vehicle is a white swan symbolizing wisdom: A swan can separate a mixture of milk and water and drink only the milk.

Fig. 5.15 Ratu Nini Besaki (viewer's left) and Ida Ratu Saung

Ratu Nini Besaki is identified with the Naga (snake) Queen, who has come from Besaki. The blood shed during cock fighting is offered to Ida Ratu Saung. Deities are invoked at this shrine for important rituals, such as Odalan (festival commemorating the temple's founding).

Fig. 5.16 View of the northwestern corner of Pura Puseh. From the viewer's left, part of Ida Tatu Saung (cf. Fig. 5.15) (1 of Fig. 5.17), Ratu Ngelurah (guardian deity) (2), Taksu (Skill Energy) (3), Gedong Tarib (4), Peliangan (5), Gedong Sari (Treasure House) (6), Ida Ratu Atma (7), Padmasana (8), Gedong Kehang (part) (9) and Pengias Agung (part) (10).

Fig. 5.17 Line drawing of Fig. 5.16

The Balinese word "taksu" is difficult to translate into English. It originally meant the seat for the interpreter of deities' words. During the ritual, Taksu descends to the medium, who, possessed, conveys to people the wishes of the deities. Deities or ancestors' spirits often possess the priest performing a ritual. The spirits then proceed to dance and sometimes to sing. The medium dances and sings in an unearthly voice. Siwa, source of Taksu energy, is the main medium-possessing deity.

"Taksu" also means artistic skill. Every artist is supposed to have Taksu in order to do creative work. Balinese believe that the world has been created by the skill of Taksu. The world is nothing but the manifestation of Taksu energy.

Fig. 5.18
Taksu Shrine. No sacred icon is found here.
There is no Taksu icon.

Fig. 5. 19
Peliangan. These stones are not linga,
although they look like Shiwa's liṅga symbol.

Fig. 5.20
Gedong Sari (Treasure House).
What look like deer horns behind the shrine indicate that the shrine has inherited the tradition of Majapahit Kingdom.

Fig. 5.21 Ida Ratu Atma (Soul Protector Queen)

5.2 Main Shrine Pengias Agung

Fig. 5.22 From viewer's left, Pengias Agung (Main Shrine of Pura Puseh), Pengaruman (Scented Shrine), Padmasana (Lotus Seat), Sumeru Moutain, and one edge of Gedong Kehen

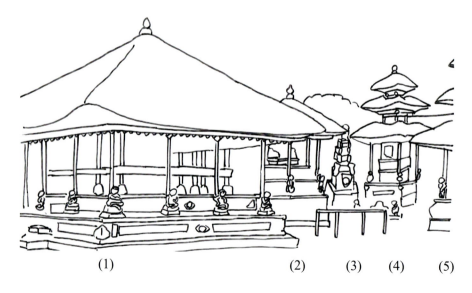

Fig. 5.23 Drawing of Fig. 5.22. (1) Pengias Agung, (2) Pengaruman, (3) Padmasana, (4) Sumeru Mountain, and (5) the edge of Gedong Kehen.

Fig. 5.24 Main shrine Pengias Agung with three paintings depicting battle between deities and demons

Fig. 5.25 From viewer's left: unidentified deity, blue Wisnu, deified Ambrosia emerging from a pot, Isvara (middle) on horseback, and Brahma. The deities are in battle with demons on Mandara Mountain. Two demons are visible at the bottom, on either side.

Fig. 5.26 From viewer's left: Blue Wisnu and his consort Saraswati, two demons (asura), and Siwa

Fig. 5.27 Here deities have succeeded in killing a demon. From viewer's left: Saraswati, Asura (demon), and Wisnu and Siwa.

Fig. 5.28 The ceiling of Pengias Agung, typical Balinese architectural style

Fig. 5.29 Center of the panel on the back side of Pengias Agung

The pot of ambrosia is depicted in the center of Fig. 5.28; above the pot are Siwa and his consort Giri Putri (Mountain-Daughter, i.e., Parvati). To the viewer's upper left, one can see the Supreme God Sang Hyang Widhi, who is also called Sang Hyang Wenang, Sang

Hyang Tunggal, or Sang Hyang Acintya.

The concept of a Supreme God is a later development in the history of Balinese Hinduism. In Indian Hinduism, belief in polytheism remains strong. The worship of Supreme Deity Sang Hyang Widhi in Bali became more dominant after Indonesian independence in 1945. The first of the Indonesian Five State Principles (Pancasila) is 'Ketuhanan yang Maha Esa,' every religious follower must worship only one Almighty God.

Bali Hindus believe that deities have their own residences. When a ritual is performed at a temple, deities are invoked by priests (pedanda or pemangku) and called to the temple. Deities are first invited to Candi Kurung (Fig. 2.49), the main entrance to the temple, and given scented offerings. Next, they are guided to several shrines, one by one. The shrines to which deities are invited differ according to the ritual.

On the occasion of the Odalan festival, for example, deities who have arrived at Candi Kurung are invited first to Ida Ratu Saung (Fig. 5.15). Then deities are invited to other shrines in the following order: Pengias Agung, Pengaruman Ratu Puseh, and Gedong Kehen. In another ritual, deities are guided in the following order: Candi Kurung, Ida Ratu Saung, Pengias Agung, Pengaruman Ratu Puseh, and Peselang (Fig. 5.51). Deities are said to change their clothes in Pengias Agung.

5.3 Scented Shrine Pengaruman

Fig. 5.30 Viewer's left: Pengaruman Ratu Puseh; from viewer's right: Sumeru Mountain, Padmasana (Skt. padma-āsana, lotus-seat), and other shrines

Fig. 5.31 The panel on the front side of Pengaruman Ratu Puseh.
From viewer's left: Wisnu, Siwa

Fig. 5.32 Kama (viewer's left), God of Love and his consort Rati, Goddess of Pleasure, reverse side of Pengaruman Ratu Puseh (cf. Fig. 5.30)

5.4 Lotus Seat Padmasana

At the northeast corner of the inner yard is an open-seat shrine called the Lotus Seat (Padmasana, Skt. padma-āsana). This shrine is dedicated to Supreme Deity Sang Hyang Widhi, a manifestation of the three main Hindu deities: Brahma, Wisnu and Siwa. The sun god Aditya, also depicted on the Lotus Seat, is another manifestation of Sang Hyang Widhi.

The name Sang Hyang Widhi appears in the work *Pūrvaka-bhūmi*, composed in the fourteenth century in Java. We do not know, however, when and where the present image of Sang Hyang Widhi was created.

Fig. 5.33 Lotus Seat (cf.Fig. 5.16)

Fig. 5.34 Sang Hyang Widhi at the top of Padmasana (cf. Fig. 5.32)

Sang Hyang Widhi is regarded in Bali as the highest among all deities. In order to protect the universe, he created deities including Brahma, Wisnu, Siwa, together with their consorts. These deities are considered to be manifestations of different aspects of Sang Hyang Widhi.

Fig. 5.35 Siwa in the center of the Lotus Seat (part of Fig. 5.32)

Fig. 5.36 Garuda (detail of Fig. 5.32)

Fig. 5.37 Turtle Badawang Nala encoiled by Serpent (naga) Ananta Bhoga (cf. Fig. 5.32)

The Lotus Seat is supported by the cosmic turtle named Badawang Nala, bound by the serpent Ananta Bhoga (Infinite Enjoyment). According to Balinese legend, an earthquake occurs whenever the supporting turtle moves. The serpent on the Lotus Seat holds the turtle so that it cannot move. Thus these two cosmic animals maintain the balance of the universe. Siwa protects people from misery caused by earthquakes. This is why he is enshrined in the Lotus Seat (see Fig. 5.34).

Fig. 5.38 Back of the Lotus Seat

5.5 Mount Meru

Mount Meru, the center of the universe, is the abode of principal deities like Siwa, Wisnu, and Brahma. Balinese believe that the Sun (Surya) turns around Mount Meru every day. Even today, many Balinese priests and their devotees often conduct a pilgrimage to Mount Semeru in East Java, Candi Prambanan in Central Java, and other places.

Fig. 5.39 Tower symbolizing Mount Meru (Sumeru)

On the walls of the second level of the tower symbolizing Mount Meru, manifestations of Siwa (Maha Deva, Iswara) are depicted (in Fig. 5.39-40).

Fig. 5.40 Maha Dewa depicted on the western wall of the second level of Meru Tower

Fig. 5.41 Iswara depicted on the eastern wall of the second level of Meru Tower

Fig. 5.42
Arjuna (viewer's right) and Karna, heroes of the Mahabharata, depicted on the western door of Meru Tower

Bali Hinduism was introduced to Bali by Mpu Kuturan and Mpu Barada, who apparently came from Java. According to Javanese tradition, Mount Meru was moved from India to Java. Later Mount Meru came to be identified with Mount Agung, the largest mountain in Bali.

5.6 Storage and Other Shrines

Fig. 5.43 From the viewer's left, Mount Meru, Gedong Kehen, and Pinkupan.

Gedong Kehen in Batuan temple is used for keeping manuscripts. It also becomes important when a ritual called Ngusaba was performed on the day of the full moon of Kliwon (around November). Ngusaba literally means 'sharpening.' The ritual is associated with

Fig. 5.44 From viewer's left: Gedong Kehen, Pinkupan, Ida Ratu Pande, and Peselang

Ida Ratu Pande, also important at Ngusaba, is dedicated to Sang Hyang Pasupati, Lord of all metal instruments. He is venerated especially on the day of Tumpek Landep, which usually falls in the first month of the Balinese calendar. During this day, metal things are honored for their power and function.

Fig. 5.45
Siwa on Nandi (cow) and his consort on a lion, on the door of Gedong Kehen.

Fig. 5.46 Guardian 1

Fig. 5.47 Guardian 2

Fig. 5.48 Guardian 3

Fig. 5.49 Guardian 4

These four guardians (Fig. 5.46-49) are found in front of Gedong Kehen (cf. Fig. 5.46).

Fig. 5.50 Pinkupan (viewer's left) and Ida Ratu Pande

Fig. 5.51 Deities depicted on Pinkupan. From viewer's right: Wisnu, Brahma, and demon

Fig. 5.52 From viewer's left, Ida Ratu Pande, a small shrine for Ida Ratu Selimpet, and the eastern gate of the temple

Fig. 5.53 Bale (hall) Peselang. One can see Gedong Kehen to the viewer's left, and the eastern gate of Batuan Temple to the right.

Fig. 5.54 Three panels in Bale Peselang (cf. Fig. 5.51). At the top of the photo one can see the image of Garuda (Fig. 5.57).

Fig. 5.55 From viewer's left: Siwa, Ponokawan (Siwa's attendant), and a demon

Fig. 5.56 Deities battling a demon. The blue deity at bottom left is Krsna.

Fig. 5.57 Indra (viewer's right) fights the demon for the ambrosia.

Fig. 5.58 Bale Peselang (viewer's left) and Bale Pelik.

Fig. 5.59 Garuda image on a beam in Bale Peselang (cf. Fig. 5.52)

Fig. 5.60 Bale Pelik. A priest recites mantras during a ritual.

Chapter 6

Pura Dalem

Offerings for Saraswati, Batuan

6.1 Pura Dalem Alas Arum

You will recall that each village (adasa adat) in Bali has three kinds of temples: Pura Desa, Pura Puseh, and Pura Dalem (see Chapter 1). The first two were discussed in previous chapters. The third kind of temple, Pura Dalem, is used for death rituals. Batuan Village has three Pura Dalems: Pura Dalem Alas Arum, Pura Dalem Puri, and Pura Dalem Sukaluwih. Originally, Batuan Village had only Pura Dalem Alas Arum, located to the south of Pura Puseh. The other two temples were built later at the eastern edge of Desa Adat Batuan (cf. Fig. 1.1).

According to the Batuan village office, there were two reasons for the addition. First, the village region had expanded, so that all villagers could no longer visit the temple easily. The second reason was the caste division. At present, people belonging to lower castes use Pura Dalem Alas Arum; those belonging to middle and higher castes, the other two pura dalems.

Fig.6.1 Entrance gate of Pura Dalem Alas Arum. Bale Kulkul (Bell Tower, cf. Fig. 2.20) is seen to viewer's right of the entrance gate.

Fig.6.2 Candi Kurung (Kori Agung). This gate is always closed (cf. Fig. 2.53).

Fig. 6.3 Yard in front of Candi Kurung (viewer's left). The small shrine in front of Candi Kurung is dedicated to Ratu Brayut Istri (see Fig. 6.4). One can see Bale Gong (Great Hall) at the right edge of the photo.

Ida Dane Mangku Kapal, Pemangku of Pura Dalem Alas Arum (see Fig. 6.10), recounted the ritual procedure:

> When I perform a ritual in this temple, I invoke deities and invite them to Candi Kurung. They are then guided to a small shrine called Pengias Alit to be adorned with nice robes, flowers, and so forth. Next, deities are taken to a larger, decorated shrine called Pengias Agung (cf. Fig. 5.21), the most sacred shrine in the temple, where they are offered gorgeous dress and the appropriate symbolic emblems. From Pengias Agung, deities are guided to Pengaruman (scented shrine) and offered incense and other scented offerings. Those deities usually dwell in the scented tower Pengaruman for three days. After the ritual is over, deities are seen off to their usual abode.

One understands from this explanation that deities are entertained at Pura Dalem as they are at Pura Puseh.

As seen in the following photos (Fig. 6.4-6), this temple is also used for rituals other than death rituals.

Fig.6.4 Ratu Brayut Istri to viewer's right of Candi Kurung. This goddess is believed to grant and protect children. She is depicted holding many children. People wishing to have a child visit this temple.

Fig. 6.5 The priest Pemangku Ida Dane Mangku Kapal performing a ritual in Bale Pesantian (Fig. 6.7). The priest is reciting Gāyatri-mantra (Ṛgveda, III.62) in Sanskrit. The girl in the red dress sitting before the priest is to be married soon. The priest performs a ritual to pray for her wellbeing happiness.

Fig. 6.6 Devotees praying for the wellbeing of the girl in the center (cf. Fig. 6.5), who is soon to be married

Fig. 6.7 From viewer's left to right: Ratu Ngurah Agung (Fig. 6.8), Pengaruman, Lotus Seat (Fig. 6.9), Penyimpanan (storage), Gedong (storage), a guardian's shrine), and Bale Pesantian

Fig. 6.8 Ratu Ngurah Agung (cf. Fig.6.7). This deity is believed to bring justice and protect people from all kinds of danger.

Fig. 6.9 Lotus Seat. The image of Sang Hyang Widhi at the top of this tower is slightly different from that in Pura Puseh (cf. Fig. 5.33). Serpent Bedawang Besuki holds the cosmic turtle as seen in Pura Puseh (cf. Fig. 5.36).

Fig. 6.10
Pemangku Ida Dane Mangku Kapal
(Pemangku Dalem of Alas Arum)

Fig. 6.11 Mrajapati, usually the place for funerals. Cremation is not performed in this shrine, but in front of the gate of Pura Dalem, outside the temple.

6.2 Pura Dalem Puri

Fig. 6.12 Candi Bentar, the main entrance (cf. Fig. 2.1) to Pura Dalem Puri.

Fig. 6.13
Two Balinese women carry offerings to the main shrine of Pura Dalem Puri. Kori Agung is visible behind Candi Bentar.

Carrying offerings on the head shows respect to deities. Offerings consist of flowers, fruit, candles, water, etc. Each offering has its own symbolic meaning. Flowers, for instance, signify purity and generosity. Offerings are placed and arranged in an offering box called Canang. The word "canang" is derived from an old Javanese word meaning beetle nut. Beetle nuts were originally presented as a precious offering to deities. The tradition of chewing beetle nuts is seen in South Asia and Southeast Asia.

People also offer fire or light, which is believed to dispel evil spirits. For Balinese, fire, the origin of Soul, is also a symbol of Sang Hyang Atma or Brahma. In daily house rituals as well as large ceremonies, water is an indispensable offering. In Bali water is of three kinds: water used by people for daily use, water (thirta) received from gods, and water prepared by priests.

Fig. 6.14 When a ritual begins, deities are first invited to Candi Kurung. Young coconut leaves are offered to please deities visiting the temple.

Fig. 6.15 Temple of Prajapati (Skt. Prajāpati). When a person dies, the Deity Prajapati asks his/her name. Each soul remains under Prajapati's protection until the time of cremation is decided. At cremation, the name of each soul is called, and the souls remain in Siwa's temple.

Fig. 6.16 Cremation in the yard of Pura Dalem Puri. Bodies are buried in this yard awaiting cremation. The body is covered with banana plants (February 2008).

6.3 Pura Dalem Sukaluwih

Fig. 6.17 Pura Dalem Sukaluwih. The Lotus Seat is seen in the center of the photo.

Fig. 6.18 Candi Bentar of Pura Dalem Sukaluwih

Fig. 6.19 The Lotus Seat of Pura Dalem Sukaluwih. The image of Sang Hyang Widhi at the top of the Lotus Seat and that of Siwa in the center of the Lotus Seat are similar to those in Batuan Pura Puseh (Fig. 5.32). The name of the deity beneath Sang Hyang Widhi is unknown.

Fig. 6.20 Kori Agung of Pura Dalem Sukaluwih

Fig. 6.21 Offerings for the dead, after recent cremation in the yard of Pura Dalem Sukaluwih

Bibliography

Davidson, Julian. *Introduction to Balinese Architecture.* Periplus Edition Ltd., 2003.
Geertz, Hildred. *The Life of a Balinese Temple.* University of Hawai'I Press, 2004.
Kramrisch, Stella. *The Presence of Śiva.* Oxford University Press, 1981
Tachikawa, Musashi and Sugeng Tanto. *Hindu Temples in a Village of Bali*. A Result of Japan Research Grant (No. 14401003), 2006.

About the Authors

Musashi Tachikawa, Ph.D.

(Harvard) is Professor Emeritus at the National Museum of Ethnology, Osaka, Japan. His publications include: The Structure of the World in Udayana's Realism (Ridel, 1980); Introduction to the Philosophy of Nagarjuna (Motilal, 1997); Emptiness in Indian Buddhism (Vajra, 2018).

Sugeng Tanto, Ph.D.

(Nagoya) is Part time Lecturer, Nihon Fukushi University, Aichi Prefecture, Japan. His publications include: A Study of Balinese Religion: Syncretistic Belief of Hinduism and Buddhism. Together with Mitsuru Ando (Aichigakuin Univeristy, 2008).